CHITON

AND

OTHER CREATURES

✿

CHITON

AND

OTHER CREATURES

❉

NICK NEELY

NEW MICHIGAN PRESS
TUCSON, ARIZONA

NEW MICHIGAN PRESS
DEPT OF ENGLISH, P. O. BOX 210067
UNIVERSITY OF ARIZONA
TUCSON, AZ 85721-0067

<http://newmichiganpress.com>

Orders and queries to nmp@thediagram.com.

ISBN 978-1-934832-49-3. FIRST PRINTING.

Printed in the United States of America.

Design by Ander Monson.

Cover image: Chitons in G. B. Sowerby's *The Conchological Illustrations or, Coloured Figures of All the Hitherto Unfigured Recent Shells*, via the Smithsonian Libraries and the Biodiversity Heritage Library.

CONTENTS

Chiton   1

Discovering Anna   5

A Guide to Coyote Management   25

Nasty   37

Slow Flame   47

Acknowledgments   55

CHITON

Along my home California coast, you may find, on the softest littoral rock, an infinite number of subtle dimples. It's as if, for eons, some ambitious soul lingered to rub first this spot, then that, until each became a smooth and nearly uniform divot. These shallow holes—catching seawater, reflecting sky and fog—are not the work of some invisible thumb, however, but of the foot of a five-hundred-million-year-old: a mollusk. They are the resting places of chiton.

Now the best way to understand a chiton (kī-tän) is to wait until sunset, flop on your belly at the sea's rocky edge, and lie quite still. Make sure it's high tide, when chitons are busiest. Then, with your ear pressed to the stone, you might hear the faint vibrations of scraping as, underwater, their rasp-like radulae rev up in their mouths and they begin to lurch forward to graze the algal fields, inch by inch. Some chitons reap "diatom scuzz," others prefer a healthy leaf of algae. All cut with precision: the outermost "teeth" of their radulae are capped with magnetite, harder than stainless steel.

Chitons are also called sea cradles, because eight calcareous plates overlap across their backs, a defensive arch surrounded by a fleshy girdle. More than nine hundred species crawl the world's shores, but they're most varied on our West Coast (and in Australia). If you're lucky, while perusing a Pacific tide pool you might chance upon a footlong, brick-red gumboot chiton, a creature lovingly nicknamed the "wandering meatloaf." This giant's leathery girdle actually wraps clear around its plates and is fuzzy to the touch: twenty species of red algae grow on its back. All of which makes me wonder if the gumboot wouldn't enjoy nibbling on itself, just a little.

Chitons are guarded, territorial. They don't like limpets, another grazer. They have light-sensitive organs, "aesthetes," in their shells—their plates are innervated—which relay signals to the region resembling a head. Some even have lens-bearing "eyes" on their backs and see shapes. Thus, when your shadow crosses, a chiton will cling fast, masquerading as rock. But should you, or a wave, catch and flip a chiton upside down by surprise, it will curl into a ball and go with the flow, tumbling away safely.

Here, though, is why it's really worth lying on your stomach: each night, some chiton species creep forward on established trails to their feeding grounds, usually no more than a few feet from their primary dimple. Out and back, they go, harvesting, and by morning return on these mucal routes to their hammocks in the stone, where they seal tight to conserve moisture. They perform these rounds for months before moving on to fresh algal pastures. Do you hear them? No one knows how they navigate, exactly, nor how they scour their pits (and some species don't). Like limpets, their secretions may dissolve the stone, before they polish off the job with their teeth. But now, again, I find myself wondering: Is the chiton's home its groove, equally a rut and a cradle? Or is it the endless forays made from this center?

DISCOVERING ANNA

As a child, I set out in search of hummingbirds. Probably this wasn't ordinary for a boy, and I was fortunate, indeed, to have come into a large and varied country south of San Francisco, a dry sea of chaparral up against—and sometimes over—the deer fence, a landscape with plenty of perches to map and explore: yellow sticky monkey flower, poison oak, coyote brush, ceanothus, and the miscellaneous exotics of the garden.

Anna's hummingbird was the species. *Calypte anna*, an abundant resident of the Pacific Slope. Even in winter, they're here, outside the rain-slithered window, hovering in the green, shifting from branch to branch to probe for insects, pillaging spiders and their stuck prey with hardly a quiver. A hardy bird. All but a few North American hummers migrate, and come spring, it's true, the orangish Allen's would arrive suddenly from Mexico to spar for territory. But he's smaller, less frequent, and, for now, another story.

Who is Anna? She was the Duchess of Rivoli, Anna Masséna. Her husband, François Victor Masséna, the duke, was an amateur ornithologist with a vast collection of exquisite bird skins that eventually included the "type specimen" of his wife's namesake. One imagines her as striking: light on her feet, a fine dancer; draped in stones that caught and refracted the candlelight of nineteenth-century France; a touch spoiled, certainly. She became the official mistress of the household to Eugénie, the wife of Napoleon III and last empress of France. Earlier, in 1828, Audubon visited Anna and observed that she was "a beautiful young woman, not more than twenty, extremely graceful and polite."

Apparently, the duchess was admired also by René-Primevère Lesson, a surgeon and naturalist, surely related vocations. It was he who named the species. In 1822, he left France to serve on a four-year trip around the world, during which he saw and described many of South America's most brilliant, pip-squeak birds. Rounding Tierra del Fuego, *La Coquille* (an apt ship name, *The Shell*) went as far north as Peru and then cut across the Pacific to Tahiti. Lesson gathered specimens of all kinds during his circumnavigation and brought them home to study, label, and slip away in drawers. For years, he labored to prepare the zoological chapters of the expedition's official record, and afterward he produced the world's first monograph on hummers: three volumes of luminous, hand-colored plates. It was in preparation for this work that he chanced upon an unrecognized skin in Duke Masséna's collection.

Hummingbirds, you should know, are found only in the New World. There are more than three hundred species, but only fourteen commonly breed in North America. Fittingly, Christopher Columbus was the first to write of them, in his diary: "Little birds . . . so different from ours it is a marvel." Not long after, Pope Leo X was presented with a preserved skin that is thought to have arrived inside a chest of curios and treasures, a gift from the King of Portugal in 1514. The bird's chin may well have been as ruby as the robes of Leo's cardinals. Europeans were captivated. They thought it half insect. *Oiseau-mouche*, the French said, fly-bird.

From the age of four or five, I kept little white jewelry boxes in a spare bureau in my room. Each full of findings: sand dollars, oak galls, feathers, owl pellets jutting with ivory rodent bones. A cabinet of curiosities, its drawers squeaking with the weight of geodes and fossils. If you have a sharp eye, these enthusiasms start to build upon themselves, or maybe it's the other way around. Soon others begin to notice as well. For Christmases: a rock tumbler, a seashell book, a chemistry kit (with beak-like forceps and pipettes), a microscope, binoculars, and many other useful tools I can no longer recall. Also for Christmas: more discarded gift boxes, each ready to be neatly packed and fitted into the display.

Calypte. It comes from a Greek root that means *to cover or conceal*, and a male Anna's hummingbird does peer out from beneath a hood, a veil of iridescent red. All hummers glow with refractive color. Their most lustrous feathers don't hold colorful pigments, only black melanin. Instead, a number of wavelengths reflect—rebound—from various depths in the feather's crystalline nanostructure so that, when the angle is just so, their crests and troughs align, synch up, "constructively interfere." These parallel strands of light are the intensification you see. Grind up this bird's iridescent plumage and just a small, ashen pile of dust will remain. When the angle of reflection is wrong, his crown looks entirely black; but if he turns and stares straight at you, then flash—like a red sky glancing off a sea. He can raise or lower his feather tracts, adjusting and directing this aggressive hue based on his mood. What is he hiding under there? His crown patch blends into his scaled gorget, which looks like chain mail guarding his voice.

In memory, I'm standing on our lawn with a view across the valley to a crest called Skyline, where the Pacific fog would pour over the redwoods many evenings and waver like a white tide. From the grass, in the late-afternoon sun, I'd watch the excursions of the male Anna's, especially his courtship dive. Only the males perform this elaborate dance, the most extraordinary of North American hummingbird displays: He rises slowly, elegantly, into the air, pausing to warble before he's lost to the viewer more than one hundred feet overhead. Too high to see, a speck in the platinum sky. Then he plummets—or rather, powers down at fifty-five wingbeats per second—

only to brake sharply in front of a perched female and sound a piercing note: a sharp pik made not with his voice, as once thought, but with his two outermost tail feathers. They cut the air like a sword. Quickly, he circles back, rises again. How many times have I watched him perform this "J-shaped dive," as it's called, this loop-the-loop before an inconspicuous female, "the object of the display" down below in our Australian bottlebrush? Hundreds. Thousands, in my mind's eye.

But what you really must know about Anna's, about the male specifically, is that he's the only North American hummingbird that truly sings. The males of other species make sharp, aggressive chip notes full of desire, and those of the other *Calypte* species, Costa's, do let forth a simple ascending-descending "song." But just Anna's have a bona fide tune, something to almost whistle along with. It's a squeaky warble, rodent-like. But I find it adorable. Even today, while walking a city street, I will hear his raspy singing, perhaps from a tree growing in a planter outside of Safeway. Any young sapling off the sidewalk might hold one belting at its tip amid the waves of traffic noise. Sometimes I'll stop midstride, point to the air, and say to a friend, "There's an Anna's." Wait a few seconds, listen. "There." I seem attuned to high frequencies, like a dog. Once you zero in on a sound, you're not likely to forget it. The key is learning that other language naturally, when you're young and receptive. I've heard it takes a teenager an average of seven times to commit something to memory. For an adult, often more than twenty.

❀

Several years ago, researchers from China ventured to California to investigate *Calypte anna*'s voice. They recorded forty-seven males in April and May at the Golden Gate Bridge, Golden Gate Park, Lake Merced, and Filoli Gardens, an old estate in the hills not far from where I grew up; a place my mother sometimes would visit for botanical watercolor classes (fine-tipped brushes, a few hairs sipping pigment). Each bird species' song has its own rhythm and syntax: in Anna's, the researchers—the listeners—found thirty-eight syllables in all, which build phrases like "bzz-bzz-bzz," "chur-ZWEE," and "dz! dz!" to name just a few. Each male knew an average of five syllables and shared some with his neighbors—the "tutors" he learned from—helping the birds to know and negotiate the ever-shifting boundaries of their territories, while shaping neighborhood dialects and the overall melody.

Of course, the genus *Calypte* also calls to mind Calypso, "she who conceals," the sea nymph who held Odysseus on the island of Ogygia for seven years. Shipwrecked and washed ashore, he didn't object to her company at first: they shared a bed. But after a while, Odysseus grew homesick and, wishing to leave, spent his days pacing the shore with tears in his eyes. Zeus sympathized with Odysseus's plight and dispatched Hermes, his messenger. When Hermes flew into Ogygia, he marveled at Calypso's garden: "Round her cave there was a thick wood of alder, poplar, and sweet smelling cypress trees, wherein all kinds of great birds had built their nests." But Calypso wasn't pleased with his tidings: she must let Odysseus go. "You gods," she cried out, "ought to be ashamed of yourselves. You are always jealous and hate seeing a goddess take a fancy to a mortal man, and live with him in open matrimony. . . . I got fond of him and cherished him, and had set my heart on making him immortal, so that he should never grow old all his days." But it was decreed. Her human must continue on.

Sixth grade brought new sophistication. My parents gave me a Nikon camera, a tool to record. Quickly I borrowed my mother's telephoto lens and stole into the brush of the backyard, into the manzanita with its small, white, bell-shaped flowers. Or I hunkered down below the prickly bottlebrush, with its myriad crimson stamens— one of the hummingbirds' favorites. My arms would grow shaky as I tried to steady the heavy lens and remain alert. Sometimes I'd lose focus, let my eyes wander. But I was always listening: bzzzzzzz. Then I held my breath, trying to still my camera and that blur of wings. Glossy prints, color slides: at night, the projector poured light through life on the white wall of my room, filling it with iridescent red and green. Click, click, I shuffled through. Many out of focus, off-center, but how could even one be thrown away? They held information. The sequence was crucial. I filed them away in plastic sheaths, in binders and boxes, as if to seal them off from dust. Someday I'd study them more carefully.

Recently, high-tech cameras helped calculate the speed of a male Anna's in his J dive: fifty-eight miles per hour. Relatively speaking, that makes him the fastest animal in the world at 385 body lengths per second—almost twice as fast as a peregrine falcon in its free-fall stoop. When a male Anna's turns in front of his female counterpart perched below, he experiences ten times the pull of gravity, more force than fighter pilots experience in their jets (they travel a mere 150 body lengths per second). The Berkeley graduate student who took these measurements, Christopher Clark, also captured a composite of one male's dive out of the blue: a long necklace of images, downstrokes and upstrokes that taper into a glide before the hummer flares its tail, braking rapidly. Calling forth.

(PHOTO BY CHRISTOPHER CLARK)

Clark journeyed to a nearby park, a retired dump—always a good place to bird—in order to perform his initial experiments on *C. anna*. He snipped the two outer tail feathers from a netted male, released it, and then watched as the bird dove: whiff. The silence astonished him. Later, he put tail feathers in a wind tunnel to further explore their "aeroelastic flutter," air trembling around those trailing vanes as if past the reed of a saxophone. He'd proven the source of the species' dive note. But in point of fact, it had already been ascertained in 1940, when another inquisitive soul mounted the outer tail feather of an Anna's on a thin strip of bamboo and, like a kid, whipped it (pik) through the air.

Slowly I discovered the males' routine singing perches. The highest lay beyond the lemon bushes, over the deer fence, and above a tangle of scrub. My father built us a tree house twenty feet beyond our latched gate, in an oak leaning precariously above a small, dusty canyon with a horse trail running through. Two parallel planks ramped up the trunk. From there, a few wooden boards nailed to the bark served as a ladder to a deck with railings. Above the ravine's steep slope, we rode currents of air. The canopy of oak leaves was our roof, broken with light, projecting green across the platform. In middle school, in pursuit of hummers, I would creep nervously out onto a twisting branch, hold tight with one hand, and with the other take photographs of a male Anna's, half in shadow, crooning at the edge of the tree. It was as if he were looking out for signs of land.

❋

Myths of origin, flights of fancy: the town where I was raised is named for Don Gaspar de Portolá, a man born in Catalonia, a soldier for the Spanish army in Italy and Portugal before he was named governor of Las Californias from 1768 to 1770. Between those years, he led a party of sixty-three soldiers and missionaries north from San Diego to establish settlements on the coast, and hopefully find Monterey Bay. Either they were unimpressed with Monterey, or they accidentally passed it by in the fog. But after three and a half months, Portolá's party came to a perch on a coastal ridge and saw a great swath of inland water. They called it *Estero de San Francisco*, thinking it an arm of the then *Bahia de San Francisco* (now Drake's Bay), so christened by another explorer in 1595. Though they didn't realize it at the time, in fact Portolá and his party were the first Europeans to glimpse what lies inside today's Golden Gate. It's funny, I could have sworn I was taught that Portolá first saw the bay from the crest of my town, but actually he summited the ridge about twenty miles farther north, as the hummer flies. This much, at least, I hope is true: Saint Francis of Assisi, the patron of my home port, once turned to his companions and said, "Wait for me here by the way, whilst I go and preach to my little sisters the birds."

In school, you are asked to relish facts, to pick apart passages, to hold them up to the light, arrange and cache them away. But they only live as you do. Not surprisingly, we often dove into California history, learning about the Franciscan missionaries, the Gold Rush, and the local Native Americans. The Bay Miwoks called hummingbirds *kulúpi*, or messenger. Their glittering feathers were woven into baskets and ceremonial headbands. Some tribes said—say—that it was Hummingbird who poked bright holes in the ceiling of night. The Ohlone, who also lived by the bay, tell of how Hummingbird's agility and cunning returned fire to the world. In the darkness, Eagle sent him on an epic mission to the underground Badger people. He was to reclaim flame for all the other animals. At his approach, the Badger people selfishly covered their glowing pit with a deer hide, but Hummingbird saw a slit of light where the arrowhead had originally passed. He poked his narrow beak through and clasped an ember, carrying the spoils away. But before he could tuck the coal under his armpit, his throat kindled and began to burn, long and slow, and even now in my backyard.

Europeans first thought the hummingbird a phoenix that could rise from the dead. The Spanish friar Bernardino de Sahagún, translating from the Aztec language in the sixteenth century, dubbed them *pajaros resucitados*—revived birds. Yet the origin of this myth is understandable: at night, or if the cold is severe, hummingbirds fall into a torpor, a temporary hibernation to save energy. The body temperature of an Anna's plunges from its normal 107 to as low as 48 degrees Fahrenheit, just enough for

life. Then, two hours before dawn, the hummer begins
to stir and vibrate its wing muscles, shivering to warm its
blood for about twenty minutes before flight. Alexander
Wilson was one of the first to note this trick in his 1831
*American Ornithology; or The Natural History of the Birds
of the United States, Volume Two.* One cold day, he prodded
a hummingbird in a shaded wire cage—not an Anna's,
but a ruby-throated, the only hummer found in eastern
North America. "No motion whatever of the lungs could
be perceived, on the closest inspection," Wilson recalled,
"though, at other times, this is remarkably observable;
the eyes were shut; and, when touched by the finger, it
gave no signs of life or motion." So Wilson carried the
bird outside and set it in the sunlight, where it must have
glowed even in stillness. He continued to watch: "In a
few seconds, respiration became very apparent; the bird
breathed faster and faster, opened its eyes, and began to
look about, with as much seeming vivacity as ever. After
it had completely recovered, I restored it to liberty; and it
flew off to the withered top of a pear tree."

Calypte. Before he left Ogygia, Odysseus confessed to
Calypso that he thought she was gorgeous, more beautiful
than his wife. Still, he wanted desperately to go home.
She sent him sailing with bread, wine, and water on a raft
he'd built from the island's largest trees. He navigated by
the stars, those holes poked in the sky. It took Odysseus
ten years, all told, to return home from Troy. Homer
doesn't mention any children between him and the sea

nymph, but other classical accounts suggest one or two. Now I find myself wondering: Did René-Primevère Lesson, upon discovering this bird new to science in the duke's collection, suddenly recall the story of the sea nymph? Did he name this beaut for Anna Masséna in patronage, or with secret affection? Did he imagine and long to see the bird floating, singing, above these green-brown hillsides of a land he would never visit?

On the fringe of Silicon Valley, in the late 1990s, we learned to make clunky websites, feeling like pioneers. Eighth grade. If my memory serves, each of us picked a different animal, and mine, of course, was Anna's. We searched field guides, textbooks, and other soon-to-be-extinct genres for vitals, and then we bracketed this natural history between simple code. Several of my best snapshots I scanned and cropped with precision; my friends, working on behalf of cheetahs and blue whales, couldn't so easily include original art. And when I walked through the tinted-glass doors of the cool, cave-like computer lab into the warmth and glare of the school's courtyard, how satisfying to hear that familiar voice from the oaks or the wisteria trained on a trellis overhead. That website is lost now, ether. I'm not entirely sure that it ever went live.

A further education: at school, there was this girl, Moriah. Several years in a row, she won a blue ribbon at our science fair for *Anna's Choice I, II,* and *III.* Her motivating questions: Does Anna's hummingbird have a feeder color preference? Do Anna's hummingbirds prefer feeders with perches? Does feeder exposure influence feeder choice by Anna's hummingbirds? Her explorations and answers didn't light my fire, but I admired and envied her immaculate poster board (fastidious, she was—or her parents) and her brilliant array of glass bottles hung upside down, each with sugar water. Anna's hummingbirds, not surprisingly, are highly territorial. I hear she's a geneticist now. It's a shame that I was too proud, or shy, to talk to her about our mutual fascination with a creature whose heart can beat over a thousand times per minute.

To know, to understand. Our desire is for more. New heights: they're always within reach. Stay, Odysseus. Several years ago, scientists anesthetized and performed minor surgery on a small flock—a hover, a glittering, a tune, a shimmer, a bouquet—of Anna's, all caught near Los Angeles. They inserted .08 millimeter silver wires into their breasts, into the pectoralis major, in vivo, and flew them in a controlled setting—inside a box— to discover, by way of electromagnetic waves relayed along the wires, how their muscles are selectively fired depending on the intensity of flight. The scientists dialed back the air density to make the birds increase their exertion and lengthen their strokes. They also put tiny harnesses around the birds' scintillating necks and attached them to weighted chains, to measure their ability to lift increasing loads. Cameras recorded it all. "These results suggest that hummingbirds recruit additional motor units (spatial recruitment) to regulate wing stroke amplitude but that temporal recruitment is also required to maintain maximum stroke amplitude at the highest wingbeat frequencies." I must confess I have only the foggiest notion of what this means; in essence, first more muscle fibers contract, and then they do so more quickly. But just imagine all those birds hovering, pulsing, at the end of their silver tethers.

Leaving a basketball game once, I spotted a male Anna's lying in the gutter among the curled oak leaves of winter. How old was I? It slips my mind. But from the rush of spectators heading toward their cars, I stepped off the curb and scavenged it with the pinch of my fingers. A little gummy mass, stuck with bits of sand, had spilled from its feathers and congealed: not an oxygen-rich red, but darkness, the way its hood and gorget look in life when the bird turns its head and the blaze disappears. I placed the bird in my palm and carried its weightless body home. It was the first time I'd held a hummingbird. On the desk in my room, I laid the specimen on a clean sheet of watercolor paper and bent my lamp low. With a black felt-tip pen, I ruled out several inches and took photographs of the bird beside the ticks of the line. I measured those wings, its compact viridescent body, its slightly decurved bill: discovered and documented such fineness. Then I set it—him, because of the scarlet crown—on a windowsill outside the laundry room, in a lidless Tupperware so air would circulate (a hint of sulfur). A few weeks later, he was gone, as if he'd flown away. I was surprisingly hurt. Sick to my stomach, even. Around and around the driveway I wandered, looking, wondering if he might have blown again to some far corner, some island or pile of leaves.

Safe passage is not guaranteed. In 1670, the governor of Connecticut, John Winthrop, delivered an emblem of the Americas to the English naturalist Francis Willughby with a note: "I send you withal a little Box with a Curiosity in it which perhaps will be counted a trifle, yet 'tis rarely to be met with even here. It is the curiously contrived Nest of a Humming Bird, so called from the humming noise it maketh whilst it flies. 'Tis an exceeding little Bird, and only seen in summer, and mostly in Gardens, flying from flower to flower, sucking with its long Bill a sweet substance. . . . I never saw but one of these Nests before; and that was sent over formerly, with some other Rarities, but the Vessel miscarrying, you received them not."

All that time I spent watching Anna's in the backyard, I never found a nest. I knew his territorial perches, each and every twig, but I was never quite on her wavelength. In contrast to the male, she is quiet, gray and green, truly concealed except for a small, irregular iridescent spot on her throat, a discreet touch of flare as if a gift from him. She is very independent: Anna's hummingbirds don't pair. The male doesn't help rear. But there's this early note, suddenly, a rekindled memory: Six or seven years old, I'm at a park when, at my feet, I chance upon a half-dollar-size nest on the lawn. A thimble of down, woven with lichen scales and spider's silk—the prize of any collection. But it never reached the bureau; it must have foundered, slipped out of my hand somewhere between the grass and the car, and I'm remembering it now for the first time in a long while.

Then this fact, not at all strange, but wonderful: in the first half of the twentieth century, Anna's didn't range north of Southern California. In winter, they wandered into Arizona, but not much farther afield. Since then, however, their numbers have boomed, right alongside California's great water projects, which gave rise to orchards, to urban and suburban gardens with flowers when all else is quiescent. Eucalyptus also proliferated, which the birds love (rightly so, since the tree shares their name, *calypte*: its tasseled flowers are well "concealed" by a hard cup). Sugary feeders grew in popularity as well. Thus Anna's irrupted elsewhere, tied to us. They've colonized the whole coast and are now across the border into British Columbia. Onward and upward, into their dive.

✿

How often our strongest memories seem to take shape at a fence line, some edge: I am standing in the lemon bushes below the adobe retaining wall of our tiered vegetable garden. The lemons are soulful, aromatic, so close their waxy, puckered surfaces fill my peripheral vision. But I'm peering through the fence's wire windows into a wash of sinuous, drought-tolerant scrub taller than me. I'm birding, I imagine—looking out for California quail or thrashers, and Anna's. Suddenly one arrives from behind, startling me. So close, the camera useless. I hold my breath as if submerged, while the hummer dangles inches from my face. I imagine its black, wiry toes clasping the freckled bridge of my nose. It twists slightly, an ornament hanging, shifting as if to see its reflection in the glistening leaves. It hangs there, in my childhood. Then whir.

As it turns out, a male Anna's dives headlong toward the sun. They have evolved to do this, we think, so that their vermilion reflects exactly into the eyes of the beloved or the intruder. The biologist who first wrote of this azimuthal tendency carried a stuffed specimen mounted on a wire into the Berkeley Hills and held it up, like a lightning rod, for the living. I imagine him crouching as a hummer bears down. "In this circumstance," wrote William J. Hamilton, "the orientation of the dive was easily determined. . . . The effect is one of a tiny ember, suddenly descending upon the observer, growing in brilliance and dimension as it approaches, to burst with a pop as it passes over." They are such jealous birds, extremely competitive. When I was a boy, three or four Anna's at a time would dart overhead, chasing each other, rattling their high-pitched calls like cans trailing from a marriage car, like sirens. They seemed to call to me as they defined and furiously defended their territories in a yard I would eventually learn wasn't really mine. Then, exhausted, that hover or shimmer of birds would fall away to separate twigs, each to sing. The Spanish, of course, gave up California. The tree house oak fell down. Our actual house was sold.

What's strange, at last, about a hummingbird is that, even as it lingers, you anticipate its departure. Sometimes this distracts you from the present. My hometown is this way, now. Small, green, zipping through. Iridescent, from certain angles. I still visit. There are still photos, boxed away, of a shadowy figure framed among the foliage. But it's unlikely I'll live there again, where the dust and amber light are so entwined as the sun lifts from the oaks and, far off, withdraws into the redwood crown of the Santa Cruz Mountains. Such is the J dive of discovery: again and again (and again), there is also loss. But more is found.

A GUIDE TO COYOTE MANAGEMENT

Coyote can be detrimental to any number of natural resources, including livestock, watermelons, pets, and the economy. He is known to tiptoe about places he shouldn't, like airport runways and Walmart parking lots.

Occasionally Coyote takes larger prey, small ungulates such as fawns, lambs, calves, and foals. The concern of this document, however, is primarily with domesticates; Bambi—another of the First People—is on his own.

Let's keep in mind that Coyote warrants management in part because he feeds on calves by eating into the anus or enteric region. The coprophagic son of a bitch absolutely loves it. He can't wait to do it again. "Up yours!" says Coyote—his mantra.

If you find a dead lamb, calf, or foal and suspect Coyote, first examine the neck and throat for subcutaneous hemorrhaging. Typically, bites to a dead animal do not cause hemorrhaging, although this diagnostic is unreliable if the carcass is old or widely scattered.

Among animal tracks, Coyote's are smaller than wolf, smaller than large dog, larger than fox, smaller than yours. His footprint tends to be more ovular and compact than dog or human; his step is light and regular, and always just ahead or just behind. Quiet, he is near.

By law you are allowed to kill Coyote year-round, if you have a hunting license. But as a gentle reminder, night-shooting Coyote with a spotlight is illegal in most states. Wait for a full moon, when he'll come creeping along like the mailman, drunk on cheap beer, pissing morning glory, looking to sleep with your daughter and your dog.

Before we go any further, remember: the focus of managing Coyote should be damage prevention and control. Termination of Coyote and his legacy is not the goal. *Coyote was here!*

To start, a good fence goes a long way against Coyote. Until he decides to go around it. Watch him tightrope the barbed wire along the highway just for show. He keeps a stepladder in his back pocket, a shovel up his coat, and the sun on his raggedy shoulders. He squats on top of fence posts, marking his miles.

His digging may be discouraged with a length of barbed wire along the ground. Climbing may be deterred with an electric overhang. With enough barb and current, anything may be deterred, maybe even Coyote. He will be kept busy scavenging the souls of other animals, such as the migrating antelope strung up across the range.

During a one-year study involving one hundred Kansas sheep farmers, seventy-nine sheep were taken by Coyote while in their corrals. He laughed all the way to the bank and thought about number eighty. Why'd he stop? Coyote despises round numbers. He hunts them in his sleep.

Yet only four of those kills occurred in lighted pens. Circling or blinking lights further increase the chances of frightening Coyote away. Alternately, use blue or red lights, because Coyote seems *less* afraid of those particular tints. Take aim as he steps into the color and begins to dance with his shadow, whispering to himself. Stay steady. Look through the sights to his stare.

Here's an idea: keep the radio playing all night. Coyote can't stand talk radio, AM especially.

But beware, he digs most music. He keeps a half-torn, life-size poster of Lil Wayne on the wall of his den. Hip-hop one day, he can be pretty darn country the next. And rock-and-roll? Of course: Coyote's always ready to kick up some dust, to howl at some tune.

Park your pickup near the corral. Park it in a new place each sundown. Coyote will wonder: what is up with that restless Chevy? If that doesn't do the trick, then spend a night in the cab. What could be better than blowing Coyote away from a blind with headlights? What could be more comfortable?

Careful, though—fall asleep, and you might wake up to Coyote's bare ass spread wide across your dusty windshield, giving birth to the bobblehead on your dashboard.

Two words: propane exploders. But make sure to turn off these noisemakers at sunrise. If Coyote is killing your sheep during broad daylight, turn to page 32.

In twenty-four Coyote depredation complaints recorded during a two-year study in North Dakota, propane exploders were recognized as most useful in reducing Coyote's antics. That is, until Coyote was simply "removed." Much more effective for a while.

But when he returned, Coyote lifted one leg and urinated exactly where he left off, in the thistle at the side of the road. His piss sprang into the air and took shape, becoming the first goldfinch. Perhaps this is why goldfinches have always flown a bit wobbly, dipping up and down like telephone wires.

Electric guards are a more expensive, even more effective option. They strobe brightly and blare horrible noises.

Place your EGs high up on posts or trees to increase the range of their effectiveness and to prevent your irritable livestock from destroying them.

Unfortunately no external chemical repellent is known to dissuade Coyote from killing a sheep. None is repugnant enough. Coyote, after all, is made of scraps of squirrel fur and glued together with piñon sap. He lost his first self, skin and all, gambling at a truck stop. It's safe to say he's made his peace with foul smells.

If an effective repellent were discovered, surely the U.S. Environmental Protection Agency would never approve it. Hell, because of the EPA, a number of useful toxicants are no longer listed here. Blame Coyote. It was Coyote who began the environmental movement. He planted the first magnolia on the original Earth Day. He has sat for centuries, waiting for it to bloom.

During a controlled study, Coyote showed some aversion to high-frequency sounds broadcasted within one foot (30 cm) of his ear.

"No shit," said Coyote, when later asked about the experience. He declined further comment. These words have often been misunderstood.

Try lacing a dead sheep with vomit-inducing salt. The technical term for this time-tested technique is "aversive conditioning." Colloquially, it's "gross." Coyote will turn mangy tail, to be sure, and trot to the edge of the field, faced squinched tight, tongue dangling. "Fuck you!" he'll yell out, and go in search of water.

Guard dogs can be effective against Coyote, depending on the terrain and experience of the dog. To raise a guard dog, select a pup from a good breed. Separate the young dog from its siblings after eight weeks and place it with sheep in a pen. Be sure escape is impossible. Let this socialization period last another eight weeks. Check the pup daily, but don't pet it. The dog's primary bond should be to the sheep. But first, before any of this, check to see that the sheep are not actually Coyote, wearing masks.

You should know, however, that guard dogs have been known to threaten children and cyclists. Consider whether you want to encourage such activity. In general, it's best to follow the ~~golden~~ rule. *What would Coyote do?*

Donkeys, also known as burros, are gradually gaining in popularity as sheep-protectors. Eventually, they may replace guard dogs entirely. A jackass's response to Coyote includes braying, exposed teeth, and a loping attack. They whole-heartedly loathe Coyote, though they are generally friendly to people. It may be because Coyote sneaks up on them through tall grass and rides them bareback.

Fact or fiction: more than one-fifth of Texan sheep and goat farmers rely on a jackass to safeguard their livelihood.[1]

Whatever. Llamas are the wave of the future. Someday they will replace donkeys as the best guard animal, because llamas befriend sheep within hours. Not surprisingly, 80 percent of ranchers who use llamas to guard their sheep are either "very satisfied" or "satisfied"—and that's the truth.

They're satisfied—are you? *Damn right—every night, for hours, if you know what I mean . . .*

No? Well, then try running your sheep and cattle together. Studies have examined the effectiveness of mixed sheep-cattle herds, and results show that Coyote kills fewer sheep. Strangely, no one knows why. Who *can* know why? Why is Coyote Coyote? *Coyote?*

The Os in Coyote are for ostrich. Let's face it: Coyote's just plain suspicious of novel, flightless stimuli. He buries his head in the sand, like the rest of us.

M-16? How about M-44. This spring-loaded booby trap shoots sodium cyanide into Coyote's open mouth when he clamps down on a baited capsule. Death occurs within seconds—dead serious. Unfortunately the effectiveness of the M-44 is hindered somewhat by EPA regulation in the interest of human and environmental safety. Additionally, it may kill your dogs.

Introducing the 1080! The 1080 Livestock Protection Collar selectively kills Coyote. Each twenty-dollar LP collar holds 300 milligrams of Compound 1080 solution. When Coyote clamps down on your livestock's jugular— ha!—he punctures the collar and swallows a lethal amount of toxicant. No, Coyote—fuck *you!*

Even better, 1080 is a slow-acting toxin. Death is prolonged. Coyote will cry. Coyote will laugh. He will watch the vultures circle to his eyes. At the end, Coyote will like the way the flies dance on his skin.

Trapping? Some people succeed, though it's a lot of work. Hope is the thought of trapping Coyote.

A short list of items needed to trap Coyote:

1. A plastic bucket to carry items 2 through 10.
2. A No. 3 or No. 4 trap.
3. One 17- to 23-inch stake for securing the trap.
4. A straight-claw hammer to carve a hole in the ground and drive the stake.
5. Leather gloves. Lord knows this is dirty work.
6. A burlap bag to kneel on for comfort. Keeps jeans clean, too.

7. Plastic sandwich bags to overlay on the earth, preventing dirt from getting under the pan of the trap.

8. A screen sifter for sprinkling dirt over the trap.

9. A rib bone—and not anything else—for leveling off the trap once set.

10. A jug of Coyote's urine to attract Coyote.

If you have allotted four hours to setting traps, devote three to looking for Coyote's signs, such as scat and tracks. Then, beat Coyote at his own game by using tricks to pique his intrigue. Place a long feather near the trap, for instance, and tickle his fancy. Or bury a ticking clock. Coyote will come around when it's time.

Don't leave scattered gum wrappers and cigarette butts. That's littering. Coyote knows it and knows better. He refuses to clean up after you.

Do place traps near carcasses or parts of animals. Leftover sheep heads are choice. Sheep heads really bring Coyote in. He's got a closet-full at home.

Check the traps every twenty-four hours. No, check that. Check them once a week and save yourself some time. Let the Old Man suffer, if he's there. Better, anyway, to spend that time making sure that your livestock is not actually Coyote.

Unless, of course, you really want to shoot Coyote in the head. Unless, of course, you really want to hear Coyote sing.

The only Coyote fumigant currently registered with the EPA is carbon monoxide. Cartridges may be purchased to toss down Coyote's burrow. Quite possibly, it's the best way to have a "little chat" with Coyote and his family. This strategy is called "denning."

In classic denning, a hunter stealthily advances downwind of Coyote's home carrying a rifle or a repeating shotgun with heavy shot. He brings a dog to distract Coyote. He makes a call that sounds like the death squeal of Coyote's children. Coyote emerges and chases his tail to within short range of the unseen hunter.

That's when you pull the trigger. Pull it twice. Shoot the shit out of Coyote. Make a machine gun sound through your teeth as you do.

Should he escape, drive stakes into the earth two inches apart at the den mouth and trap his pups. If he returns, shoot him, and then destroy his young. If Coyote does not return soon, destroy the pups anyway. Predation will often cease when the young are lost.

Where aerial shooting is legal and the den is in open terrain, wait until Coyote's little ones venture outside to frolic and doze in the sun for the first time, then decimate Coyote and his progeny all at once, like a hailstorm from an empty sky. Think "video game."

Denning is cost-effective. Bullets are cheap. Coyote will sell them to you in bulk. I mean come on, now. Don't be a sucker: can't you see it was Coyote who invented the gun?

---

[1] Answer: Coyote wrote the question.

NASTY

I'm loitering in the dark with two strangers, Dominican brothers fishing at India Point Park on the waterfront of Providence, Rhode Island. All in our twenties, we watch, momentarily, as a stray tabby cat and its streetlight shadow explore a yawning hole in a rusted-out garbage can. The head of Narragansett Bay, the state's lifeblood, stretches behind us. Orange and white lights waver at its edge. Suddenly, the younger brother—Eduardo is his name—has something on his line, and we turn back to the water. His hands leave his pockets and fumble for the rod as it rattles against the railing.

"A small one," Eduardo says, after the initial jolt, disappointment in his voice and shoulders. "Another schoolie." But I'm always curious to see a fish.

His line swerves, trembles. It glints in the periphery of the park's glow, cutting across the black of the bay. Eduardo draws up and reels, turning slightly on his hips. His catch thrashes as it approaches. We hear anonymous splashes. Then quiet. I think it's lost, but it's only gone deep. One final dive before the rush to surface.

When the water breaks again, Eduardo raises an

American eel: roughly two-and-a-half feet long; one roiling, arm-like muscle. Small, but strong. Fighting hard. All resistance. The three of us recoil as it comes wriggling over the railing. Apparition. A glimpse of underworld. The creature is amazing as it panics, swirling and suffocating in midair.

We panic, too, in our way. "Fucking shit," says Alexandro, Eduardo's older brother, both amused and appalled. He and I skip back a few steps, clearing space, while Eduardo pushes his rod as far as possible from his torso. Rigidly, as if the thing is contagious, he cranes the eel over the railing and lets it drop in the grass.

"We got to cut the head off," Alexandro says. Good brotherly advice. On the lawn, the eel reminds me of a violin: alternately shaping each f-hole as it flails—back and forth, back and forth—and somehow also the string. But the eel is soundless, except for the swish of its body on grass. I am silent too, but for a few unconscious groans and hums. Like the brothers, I'm at once attracted to and repulsed by this creature; emotions as indistinct, from a certain distance, as the poles of an eel's body.

"With scissors?" asks Eduardo.

"Oh yeah, with scissors," says Alexandro. "For sure. These things . . . these things are *nasty*."

He shakes his body, half instinct, half theater.

"Nasty!"

❊

As if warming his hand above a fire, a man named
Tommy readies himself over his quivering rod. It's
a cold early morning. He and a friend, David, are just
off the night shift, fishing clam worms under the I-95
bridge that crosses the salty Seekonk River. This is the
city of Pawtucket, five miles north of India Point, where
the Narragansett narrows to a stone's throw. By mid-
morning, the tide will ebb and these men will be asleep.

"Nah," Tommy says, relaxing again in his thick coat.
"Just current." But, another tremble. A decided shake.
David looks on.

"Never mind," admits Tommy. "There's something.
But I'm going to wait." Sometimes it's best to let a fish
hook itself. Let it swallow the bait.

"Pick it *up*," says David. "Come *on*."

"Nah, it's just biting around the edge. If it were large,
it would take the whole thing. If it's a small one, I don't
want it anyhow."

"Why not?" David asks. They haven't hooked even a
small one this morning. David has a point. So Tommy
sets it with a swift, pirouetting yank.

"On?" asks David.

"Yup. But it's baby."

It's an eel, actually. A glistening yellow belly, a slate-
green back. Tommy lifts it from the water and lets it
down in the dirt below the bridge. We watch it roll, in

frantic waves. David gives a hoot and pretends to run away, lifting his knees high as if in fright. The fish has swallowed the hook entirely; thin, clear monofilament runs from its mouth like a tongue. No one moves to touch it.

"Just look at that," I say, standing with Tommy over the eel. Even on this foreign stage, the sheer speed, the sinuosity, of its athleticism is captivating, metronomic—an unfortunate misunderstanding. How accidental that this found Tommy's worm on the dark bottom; that the eel swallowed it whole; that such a creature evolved to root through mud, the nooks and crannies of the estuarine floor. It is an animated intestine. Watching the eel struggle, I long to see one on its own terms—an improbable wish.

"Will you use it for bait?" I ask.

"This thing?" Tommy raises his eyebrow skeptically. "Don't think so."

"That fuck'n eel is *nasty*, dog!" David bellows. He hops about in anxious excitement. He takes a photo of the fish with his cell phone and shows Tommy immediately, as if to verify its existence. Tommy squints at the tiny, pixilated image. Or cringes. Then he hoists the grit-covered eel back over the railing and dips, letting us all breathe.

"It just wants to sink to the bottom," Tommy says, lifting it again. The eel is clean now. Elastic as a bath toy. Reluctant to let his fingers near the eel's mouth, Tommy slips on David's yard gloves to unclasp the leader, fish and all, above the river. When he manages, it dangles like a Christmas ornament from his hand. Like a stocking from its own loose end.

"Want it?" he calls down the railing, to be neighborly. Two other fishermen shake their heads.

"I'm gonna let it go right from here, give it a chance," Tommy says. And he does. "Maybe the hook'll rust out."

Along River Drive, another stretch on the tidal Seekonk between India Point and Pawtucket, a man named Miguel, wearing sweatpants and a white tank top, fishes with his two sons after dark. He has hulking, sculpted arms. The children spot a rat scurrying through the cracks of the riprap. The little one is afraid of the motion, the quickness.

"Do you like to fish?" I ask the older boy, as his brother plays with plastic toy trucks in the rutted dirt between the street and the river.

"Yeah," he says. "I don't eat them. But, yeah."

"Why not?"

"Um . . ."

"You don't like to eat fish?"

He hesitates, rubs his throat. He's about nine or ten.

"My dad," the kid says, "he cuts the head off and the blood . . ."

His voice trails off, like the words are caught. Too personal. Pulling his chin to his neck, the boy makes a face and raises his hands, as if to rid them of a thing they've felt.

"The other day, my dad caught a blue one," he goes on. He means a bluefish, which is what people primarily fish for on the Seekonk River. That and striped bass. "Right away, he cut the head," says the boy. "I don't like to see. It's nasty."

Twenty minutes later, Miguel drags a petite eel through the reeds of the shallows, the smallest I've ever seen at the end of a line. The kids move in to take part in the landing. I follow, too. A friend of Miguel's helps hold it, as the children and I watch, wide-eyed. Deep in its throat, bulging, is the hook, like the lump of a mouse in a snake.

"Guys," Miguel says firmly, "go over there for a second." The older boy looks to his father. Then he puts his arm around his younger brother and leads him away. They wander down the bank, reluctant, eyes trailing.

Slipping a pocketknife from his baggy sweats, Miguel stabs the eel beneath its peanut-shell jaw. Blood runs black in the dim light down his strong hands. The fish slows. Stops. With a pull, Miguel removes the hook and strides off after his boys, while his friend wraps the small, glistening eel in a rectangle of used tinfoil, carefully folding the crinkled silver over its pencil-body and crimping the edges.

The eel still writhes on the grass at India Point Park. Eduardo, Alexandro, and I circle around. Three young men unnerved by a fish. Such power in form.

"I've heard they're good to eat," I offer.

Though true, these words seem absurd, ridiculous, in the moment. Eduardo and Alexandro are incredulous. How do you eat this shapeshifter, this slippery energy?

Alexandro moves to a picnic table, rifles through a tackle box. "Take it over there, under the light," he directs. Dutifully Eduardo lifts the rod, carrying it to a bike path where he sets the dangling eel beneath the electric hum of a streetlamp.

"You want it?" Alexandro asks me, in the sterile fluorescence, as he strides up with a large pair of scissors.

"Want it?"

"Want to keep it?"

"You won't eat it?" I ask.

"Hell no," Alexandro says.

"Too much work, anyway," adds Eduardo. "Too hard to peel off the skin. You have to peel it off like a sock."

A strange desire washes over me. It is long, like an arrow, with a translucent, narrow dorsal fin for fletching. Delicate, fan-like pectorals hang as if vestigial from the eel's sides. A moment ago, it was an undulating ribbon in the bay. Now it swims in place, on pavement. Briefly, I imagine taking this fish home with me. I could coil it in a glass pie plate, slide it into the oven and, bite after salty bite, devour it with fork and knife, tasting the Sargasso Sea where all eels are conceived. Or, I could slip it into my housemates' beds: surprise, guys.

"No," I answer, finally. "I won't eat it." But perhaps

that would do right by this eel: to be consumed like the normal fish; to be included in the rituals that bear us along—eating, touching with bare hands.

As the brothers talk out a plan, sand on the path scours the protective film of the eel's skin and sticks. Eduardo then steps on it, pinning it down. Scissors in hand, Alexandro kneels. The hook is large and juts menacingly from its lip. I steel myself.

But when he begins, Alexandro only uses the tool like pliers to pry out the hook. He spares this fish, though perhaps its crucial moment has already passed. As Alexandro struggles quietly, red glazes the raised pebbles of the concrete in visible spurts.

When the hook finally retreats, and the eel is released from its hold, it signs a frantic figure eight in rapid stages, first S-ing one way, then the other, over and over. It reverberates like a windmill—the type that resembles a giant eggbeater, blades whirring on a vertical axis. It rotates, rotates, rotates, while there's still breeze.

Eduardo scavenges a paper napkin from the grass nearby. Bending, he grasps the eel's neck and walks briskly toward Narragansett Bay with an outstretched arm. Short of the railing, he stops. He straddles his legs, draws the fish back and, as if a kid flinging a branch alone in a forest, lets go. The eel swings end over end, and cracks somewhere below on the water. The white napkin returns to the ground in a flutter.

I ask if it will survive, but know. They shrug.

We scan for signs. Only waves catching the streetlight.

"Now *that's* nasty," Eduardo says, pointing behind us. We turn, again. Back on the path, the tabby and another cat are on their haunches, licking blood under the light. Licking it all up, hungrily, beside the rod.

The first is severed six inches below its head. Iridescent black flies swarm both halves of its body.

The second is wrapped in lime-green fishing line, its tail tucked beneath a rosy towel aside a yellow Solo cup. Bits of broken glass adhere, and glittering sand.

The third rests on a rumpled scrap of black canvas— an old tent, I think, still with a few aluminum poles, left by someone homeless. This eel is a foot long, maybe less, and curled through the hoops of a six-pack's plastic.

One more: a perfect, frozen S. Two flies work its mouth. Its pectorals remind me of ears set too far back on a head, or of buttresses holding up a cathedral. A nearby McDonald's cup mimics its body: tipped over, red straw bent at a wild angle.

Even in death, eels seem to smile. BB-black eyes. Tails like oversized butter knives. Their skin: leather on a dark sofa, tightening. Ribs beginning to show. Beneath I-95 again in Pawtucket, I find them together on the granite river wall above the Seekonk.

"They're nasty-looking, aren't they?" a passing fisherman says, suddenly disturbing my examination. I nod in agreement: not because they look or feel alien to us, but because they were left here, disfigured, to dry among our trash.

"If they wanted to kill them," he goes on, "I don't understand why they didn't just cut them up, throw them back into the water."

I nod. "Why not throw them back alive?" I say.

"I was here yesterday evening, and there was only one," the fisher says, nodding. "Three must have been last night." Eels are most active in the elements we fear.

When I lift the first, the flies fall away. The eel stinks, but its rubbery skin is oddly gratifying to my thumb and forefinger. One by one, I hold them up and let them drop. They sink straight and quick. It feels good to put them back. Maggot eggs float to the surface from their mouths in creamy clusters, like miniature bubbles. The flies circle back to attend to the wet stains, where eels lay.

The river, I think. The river will eat the nasty.

SLOW FLAME

Once, in Northern California, she and I were walking through a redwood park with old-growth trees, when we heard something up a side canyon, a kind of whispering. Curious, we walked up the draw along a deer trail and discovered a wildfire burning unannounced in the forest, a line of flame hardly wider than my hand. It was windless and quiet—not even the sound of wrens—and the fire was moving a few inches at a time. You could stand there and watch it come forward as if it were creeping on its belly, and I remember thinking: even a newt could outrun this.

There is a canyon next to my old home south of San Francisco, one among many, and as in most canyons, the legacy redwoods were cut a century ago. The massive stumps remind of wrecked ships. But a few great trees remain higher up, still clinging to the steepest ground, the most difficult to cut. Almost all of them are fire-scarred: their fibrous bark singed, or their hearts fully hollowed and charred. Redwoods survive fires because their wood is saturated with tannins, a fire retardant and also a mild poison, which gives them their sunset interior.

In this forest and the surrounding oak woodlands, during certain times of the year, one can find California newts, *Taricha torosa*, ambling carelessly, it seems, in all directions. They are the color of decaying needle: deep brown on top, their underbellies a brilliant orange. They hatch in cold creeks and ponds, where for a time they have feathery external gills, but they become terrestrial during the late summer, walking off into the duff in search of bloodworms and sowbugs. At the first hard rain, they return to their natal waters to spawn and, each winter, a few adults returned to our concrete basement, to the flooded drain where they were born.

When threatened by a prodding finger, *Taricha* newts curl their tails over their granular backs in an arch, an act as sensual as it is intimidating. When I was young, I wondered why I never found their bones in the pellets of the great horned owls roosting in the shadows of certain trees, but it's not because they seem to have none: their skin carries a poison, *tetrodotoxin*, hundreds of times more potent than cyanide. Easily enough to kill a grown human, if you were to swallow one and keep it from wriggling back up into the light. So they flash their golden undersides as if to say, Wash your hands, wash your hands. Only garter snakes, with a red stripe down their backs, have evolved immunity. They strangle and gulp newts whole.

Newts belong to the family *Salamandridae*, and in the occult, the salamander is believed to have a unique connection to fire and, thus, medicinal properties.

Aristotle wrote, "And the Salamander shows that it is possible for some animal substances to exist in the fire, for they say fire is extinguished when this animal walks over it." Pliny the Elder concurred: "This animal is so intensely cold as to extinguish fire by its contact, in the same way that ice does." Their glistening skin does suggest an immense wetness. And as newts and salamanders often hide or hibernate in logs, probably they are sometimes found near or among the ashes of a hearth. I have never seen such a thing, but I have found snakeskin in a woodstove, its broad belly scales glowing like windows.

One year our basement flooded during a heavy December storm. My mother enlisted us to help mop up the rain that was seeping in, somehow, through the walls; the same rain that was also feeding a hidden pool, the perennial source of young newts that would stumble inside and wander the concrete. A thick blue carpet was sopping, as heavy as stone and destined for the dumpster, while the skirt of an old couch wicked water toward its cushions. A mop already leaned against one wall, and, when I lifted it, newts came tumbling out of the woolly dreadlocks, plopping quietly. But not all of them: we had to shake out others that clung to these coils of moisture like children to a mother's hair.

When they landed squirming on the concrete, they turned over so lazily, almost reluctantly, and returned to their feet. Began to pace. Over the years, I would carry them outside by the handful, most of them first-year newts, about two-inches long and known as "efts." As a child, to hold one in your hand is to imagine holding a newborn. Even as an adult. The peculiar softness of it, the pinky quality, their slow motions. Momentarily your hand becomes a womb in which you hold a memory or premonition of your own evolution.

Inevitably I would forget to check the basement and some would desiccate. The moisture run out. In a desk drawer in my former room there is a tiny white jewelry box, made of cardboard, that perhaps once belonged to my mother. Inside I gathered the dead like potpourri, this beautiful "rotten" flesh. Through their parchment skin, you can see the bracelet of their spines. Only the faintest of smells, something like the apricot scent of the chanterelle slices we dried each winter. I stole them from the basement and shut them up in my cardboard sarcophagus, occasionally lifting the lid to look in. As if to see if they were ready to rise and go, back to the redwoods. *Taricha* in fact means "mummy," their name likely inspired by their warty appearance in life.

I remember one particular year finding newts squashed by the dozen on the road leading to our house. It was just as I became aware of their existence, and mainly I recall feeling helpless to save them, to stand guard long enough. Pressed to the pavement like giant worms, their pygmy limbs and jaws were identifiable among the otherwise freeform S of their bodies. There are particular roads in Northern California that, thankfully, close each year to cars during the newt migration, including one famous stretch in Tilden Park of Berkeley from November through April. Yellow "Newt Crossing" signs—a black, curled silhouette floating at center—also go up to caution mountain bikers to slow. But newts know no boundaries, and if the rains come in October, they begin to plod before the cars are outlawed. I've read of one man who, at six each morning, would ride his bike, like a boy on an early paper route, to see if the newts were shining on the road. To carry them across, in their direction.

Shortly after we met, she and I visited my hometown together. It was early January, and we decided to take a walk one night in the rain. Above the redwoods, we came to a small, lush meadow where the jeep tracks ran with rivulets and newts. Extrapolating from our flashlight beams, thousands lay in the dark wetness. Trying to find each other. Pacing with cinnamon eyes. My approach was to examine the patch where my foot would fall and then move forward confidently. But further up the hill, when I looked back, there she was, frozen, scanning the ground around her as if a newt might dash under her boot and she could never forgive herself. I had to go back and retrieve her, take her hand, convince her that the newts would survive.

More recently, but years ago now, we lived off the grid in the woods of Oregon for several seasons. We were still young in our relationship then, younger. No other lights in the valley, few visitors. She painted each day and I made attempts at writing, often staying up late into the night by the thrumming woodstove. Not far up the hill from our meadow was an artificial pond where *Taricha* newts swam lazily along the weedy edge. These were the California newt's closest cousin, the rough-skinned, *granulosa*. When both species enter their breeding waters, their skin becomes smooth, losing its warty texture. Their tails grow long and thin to serve as a propeller and rudder. They glide in casual circles and dive into the muck ahead of their corkscrewing tails. Looking down from the bank into the pond, we thought them like bathers in a park.

We swam in the pond on the hottest days and, as caretakers, once we waded in and tore out the sharp aquatic grass encroaching around its edges. Occasionally we would see a couple in the shallows in amplexus, a word that means "an embrace." He grasping her from behind, rubbing her snout with a gland below his chin. They drift together untethered. The male develops "nuptial pads," which look like black thimbles on his sixteen fingers, to improve his chances of holding onto her. For she might squirm away, never to be seen again. We had missed the season, but, earlier in the spring, wild clusters of newts can be found, a mass of males all competing for a single female somewhere in the slimy fray.

The pond was decades old and originally subsidized by the Forest Service so that, in case of wildfire, one of their helicopters could dip a massive bucket on a chain and swing up with water. All those years, the water had only ever fed the homestead's garden; our tomatoes were nurtured by the newt's algal pool. But last summer, the steep drainages finally burned, over a hundred thousand acres across the river. The river canyon, as we knew and came to admire it, was rewritten in a week's time. The cabin hillside was spared, but I am left imagining newts by the hundreds raining into the fir below the whirring blades, beside each other: their bellies the color of the conflagration, their movement in free fall a kind of slow flame.

ACKNOWLEDGMENTS

Thanks to the following publications in which these pieces originally appeared:

The Threepenny Review: "Chiton" (2015)
The Southern Review: "Discovering Anna" (2015)
River Teeth: "A Guide to Coyote Management" (2010)
CutBank: "Nasty" (2013)
The Harvard Review: "Slow Flame" (2014)

Thanks to Amy Benson, who helped inspire three of these pieces; to Christopher Coake, who helped with the other two; and to Emily Nemens and Stephen O'Connor, for their attention to "Discovering Anna."

Thanks to all my literary friends and professors at Brown University; the University of Nevada, Reno; Hunter College; and Columbia University.

Thanks to the Margery Davis Boyden Wilderness Writing Residency, the Djerassi Resident Artist Program, and the Sitka Center for Art and Ecology for supporting my writing and offering me unbelievable landscapes to explore.

Thanks to the staff of New Michigan Press and *DIAGRAM*, and especially to Ander Monson for his design work and boundless energy.

Finally, thanks to my wife, Sarah, and above all, to my parents for always encouraging my interest in creatures, essays included.

NICK NEELY grew up south of San Francisco, in the oak and chaparral on the bay side of the Santa Cruz Mountains. He holds an MA in Literature and Environment from the University of Nevada, Reno, and MFAs in nonfiction and poetry from Hunter College and Columbia University. His literary work has appeared in journals such as *Kenyon Review*, *The Threepenny Review*, *The Southern Review*, *The Missouri Review*, *FIELD*, *Ninth Letter*, and *Ecotone*. He is the recipient of a Margery Davis Boyden Wilderness Writing Residency, a UC Berkeley-11th Hour Food and Farming Journalism Fellowship, and the 2015 John Burroughs Nature Essay Award. More of his work can be found at www.nickneely.com.

❈

COLOPHON

Text is set in a digital version of Jenson, designed by Robert Slimbach in 1996, and based on the work of punchcutter, printer, and publisher Nicolas Jenson. The titles are in Futura.

✽

NEW MICHIGAN PRESS, based in Tucson, Arizona, prints poetry and prose chapbooks, especially work that transcends traditional genre. Together with DIAGRAM, NMP sponsors a yearly chapbook competition.

DIAGRAM, a journal of text, art, and schematic, is published bimonthly at THEDIAGRAM.COM. Periodic print anthologies are available from the New Michigan Press at NEWMICHIGANPRESS.COM.